Omnibus Press Presents the Story of

evanescence

by Simon Moore

Written by **Simon Moore**
Picture research, cover and book design by **Sarah Nesenjuk**

ISBN 0-8256-2994-2
Order No. OP 50666

Exclusive Distributors:
Music Sales Corporation
257 Park Avenue South, New York, NY 10010 USA

Music Sales Limited
8/9 Frith Street, London W1D 3JB England

Music Sales Pty. Limited
120 Rothschild Street, Rosebery, Sydney, NSW 2018, Australia

Front Cover: **Kevin Estrada/Retna**
Back Cover: **Kevin Winter/Getty**

Photo Credits:
Carlo Allergri/Getty: 74 • Awais/LFI: 49 • Robyn Beck/Getty: 82
Frederick M. Brown/Getty: 76 & 80 • Sarah De Boer/Retna: 9 • David Decoteau/Getty: 54
Scope Features/LFI: 26, & 47 • Simon Frederick/Getty: 3 • Jo Hale/Getty: 52
Dave Hogan/Getty: 50 • MKO/Cyberimage/LFI: 63 • Jen Lowery/LFI: 23, 58 & 69
Hector Mata/Getty: 30 • Frank Micelotta/Getty: 1, 7 & 51 • Jim Mosenfelder/Getty: 70
Jeff Moore/LFI: 21, 34 & 56 • Donald Weber/Getty: 92
Frank White: 4, 13, 15, 19, 20, 24, 28, 29, 39, 45, 53, 54, 55, 64, 65, 67, 85 & 91
Kevin Winter/Getty: 14, 36, 41, 60 & 87 • Ron Wolfsom/LFI: 10

Printed in the United States of America
By Vicks Lithograph and Printing Corporation

Visit Omnibus Press at www.omnibuspress.com

Omnibus Press Presents the Story of

evanescence

OMNIBUS PRESS
LONDON · NEW YORK · SYDNEY

Table of Contents

*E*vanescence's innovative, progressive sound juxtaposes heavenly, soaring vocals with hard-hitting guitar and introduces orchestral, choral, and electronic elements to driving rock. Epic, dramatic, dark, and lush: Here is a unique brand of music that unabashedly combines genres to present the most sonically compelling and creative popular music to come along in far too long.

Evanescence burst onto an unsuspecting music scene at the beginning of 2003 with their explosive debut *Fallen,* an album that was destined to go multiplatinum many times over and top charts worldwide. An ambitious, far-reaching headlining tour that was to last some eighteen months brought the live Evanescence experience to all corners of the globe. Soon the band that had emerged out of nowhere had earned themselves a loyal and ever-growing fan base as diverse as they come.

The band's meteoric rise is all the more impressive considering its humble beginnings fueled by a powerful musical vision. In a music-industry fairytale, the teenage songwriting partnership forged by lead singer Amy Lee and guitarist Ben Moody culminated in rip-roaring success while the band held on tight to its integrity and artistic ideals. Here is the magical story of Evanescence...

Origin

Not many rock stars can boast a less glamorous kick-off to worldwide success. To document the inaugural moment of Evanescence, we must travel back in time to a gymnasium in Little Rock, Arkansas, in the mid-1990s. Amy Lee and Ben Moody, whose musical partnership would generate one of the top rock acts of the new millennium, met at summer camp when the future frontwoman was a year younger than 14-year-old Ben. Amy, the new kid in town, was keeping herself company in the corner, playing piano, and just happened to be picking out the melody of Meatloaf's "I'd Do Anything for Love (But I Won't Do That)" when local boy Ben perked up his ears and made his way across the room. "I don't think either of us really fit in that well, and possibly that's what drew us together," Amy would years later tell none

other than MTV on June 13, 2003. "We were both musicians out of our element in this silly camp environment."

The two formed an instant bond over their musical tastes and interests—wide-ranging though they were. Their combined list of favorites included Portishead, Metallica, Sarah McLachlan, Nine Inch Nails, Michael Jackson, Enigma, Soundgarden, Stevie Wonder, Sting, Smashing Pumpkins, and film-soundtrack composer and former Oingo Boingo front-man Danny Elfman. Suddenly, Little Rock seemed a little more interesting to Amy, and she began spending all her free time at Ben's house where the new friends conceived a songwriting partnership that would stand the test of time and prove to be far more than an after-school distraction. "A day in my high-school life was going to school, not liking it, racing home, and trying to convince my parents to let me spend the rest of the day at Ben's parents' house ... every single day, that was what I wanted to be doing," Amy told New Zealand magazine *Rip It Up* in its August/September 2003 issue.

Both Amy and Ben had been musically minded from a young age. In his early teens, Ben could be found at Little Rock's Seventh Street Peep Show every Monday night for a sort of open-mic night where local bands signed up to hone their performance skills in front of their peers. The $1 cover charge and cheap pizza made the venue a popular hangout for the young crowd. Guitar wasn't his first love; he was originally a drummer, but due to a case of carpal tunnel he switched over to the axe—a $50 pawnshop special. He soon realized his affinity for the instrument and splashed out on the real thing: An Ibanez with a Peavey amp. Amy, on the other hand, favored the more serious side of the musical spectrum, and had nine years of classical piano training under her belt, as well as an active interest in school choir. Amy told *Rip It Up*, "I've always been partial to classical music, especially really old choral music. I think my favorite piece of music, probably, of all, is Mozart's *Requiem*." She had also, at age 11, discovered grunge. "My family moved all the time, and I really related to the lyrics, because I felt isolated and alone," she told *Rolling Stone* in its March 10, 2004, issue. The pair of new friends also had musical fathers in common. Ben grew up listening to his dad's band—that had a respectable gig schedule playing covers in local bars—practicing until all hours. Amy's dad was a radio DJ, and had introduced her to live rock by taking her to a Three Dog Night concert.

The two friends' musical backgrounds may have varied, but they both exhibited a certain, shall we say, dramatic bent early on. "I was always a drama queen," Amy happily admitted in a May 29, 2003, interview with VH-1. "I remember playing in the kitchen, trying to get my mom to think I was dead and call the police. When she didn't, I would cry. I was always theatrical. I don't think any of my relatives are surprised. When we were younger, Ben would come over and I'd come down the steps wearing some huge petticoat that I stole from school." Ben candidly disclosed to New Zealand's *Crème* magazine in a September 2003 interview. "When I was a kid I was just so obnoxious because I just loved being the center of attention, so I love being on stage. It's just the greatest feeling."

Amy kept her dramatic side a bit of a secret, however, immersing herself in arts classes and choir. "I definitely have always been an outsider, but I wasn't dressed in black all the time, slitting my wrist in the corner, cutting myself. Never! I wasn't that person. I was definitely on my own a lot," Amy, who was raised mainly in Florida but whose family moved around quite a bit, told *Launch.com* in a November 16, 2003, interview. "I was an advanced art student, and like, really into it. Like, I would just go in the hall every lunch and just be making pieces of art. Or I was choir president. You know, I was a dork. But not in the way of, 'She's one of the nerds.' It was more like, 'Who?' I really just made a big effort to dress down, and I didn't talk to a lot of people. I had one or two intimate friends, and that was it."

Vision

*A*my and Ben's creative joint venture soon took on a decidedly ambitious bent. The two young songwriters had a very definite vision, and although they had neither the means nor the resources to create the sound they had in mind, they began putting together a soundscape of vast proportions. Vibrant string sections and choruses courtesy of full choirs may not have been physically present in Ben's basement, but that didn't worry the Lee/Moody force. They set about conjuring it all up in their heads, and then got to work attempting to craft it with the meager studio gear they had at hand.

"As ridiculous as it may sound," Ben told *Guitar One* magazine in June 2003, "When Amy and I started writing together, it was just like, 'Okay,

this is what I was born to do; one of my purposes in life is to make music
with Amy.'" It was very much an exclusive musical relationship. Ben
would later reflect to MTV on June 13, 2003, that he and Amy kept
Evanescence as just the two of them because they "didn't want to bring in
all these people who were permanent members because then they'd want
to write, and that was just too complicated for us." Amy told *Guitar One*
magazine in its June 2003 issue, "Ben's the only person that I'll collabo-
rate with, writing-wise. Somehow we know where the song is headed
within the other person's head. I don't know how, and I really don't think

that's possible with anybody else." Ben stated in the band's official bio,
"We have the same exact vision regarding what we love about music.
When it comes to songwriting, we finish each other's thoughts."

   The two realized that they were well on the way to truly creating something, and decided the project needed a name. Looking for interesting
words in the dictionary, they came across one that fit. Evanescence, the
act or state of gradually fading or vanishing away—disappearance; as, the
evanescence of vapor, of a dream, of earthly plans or hopes or of the
morning mist.

Scraping together recording equipment in order to build a home studio at Ben's house, the two began experimenting with making demos. Word of an inventive new local band began to get around as Little Rock radio stations KABF and KLEC took to playing the seven-minute track "Understanding" which was also featured on a CD sampler packaged in an issue of indie music mag *Ricochet*. Evanescence songs began finding their way onto compilations courtesy of BigWig Enterprises, Flaming Fish Music, and True Tunes Music.

Evanescence began to develop a following and an enigmatic reputation.

Amy and Ben organized live shows at local venues Juanita's and Vino's and at Little Rock's River Market and the TNT Powerhouse. Vino's, a corner pub that boasts its own microbrewery and a self-proclaimed reputation as "Arkansas' premiere alternative entertainment venue" and Juanita's, a Mexican restaurant offering up live music seven nights a week, are both still musical mainstays in Little Rock. Rumors abounded as to the elusive nature of the band. Evanescence's very occasional gigs—sometimes as infrequently as a couple of times a year—managed to create an intense air of mystery around the band. It was a prime example of the effectiveness of playing hard to get, however, it wasn't by design; Amy and Ben simply couldn't afford to perform live. Their rare live appearances were patched together with as many additional musicians that they could cajole into learning the parts and playing for cash and a few free dinners.

Nonetheless, an Evanescence concert became a much-anticipated event, and the band used the exposure to sell their self-released recordings. The first such recording was an EP simply entitled *Evanescence* which the band made available at a show at Little Rock's Vino's in either December 1998 or January 1999, as per conflicting early reports. The very limited run of 100 copies featuring black and white artwork depicting a statue of a winged angel sold out that very night. The CD-R had seven tracks: "Where Will You Go," "Solitude," "Imaginary," "Exodus," "So Close," "Understanding," and "The End." Guest musicians on the EP were drummer Matt Outlaw, and, rather coincidentally, two future Evanescence band members, William Boyd on guitar and bass and Rocky Gray on drums.

That summer Amy and Ben offered up an even rarer recording, the August 1999 *Whisper/Sound Asleep* EP. Sans artwork, the 50-copy run in its clear plastic jewel case featured the original and a new version of "Understanding" along with four new songs, "Give Unto Me (Sound Asleep)," "Whisper," "Forgive Me," and "Ascension of the Spirit." Local radio picked up on "Give Unto Me" and the band's popularity in Little Rock continued to develop.

These first recordings, which today now and then surface on eBay for exorbitant sums, exhibit a bare bones version of what Evanescence was to become. Amy and Ben had a very well defined image of the music they wanted to create. As Amy would years later tell the *Washington Post* in its September 12, 2003 edition, the songwriting duo's early music "sounded different because we didn't have the means to make it sound like we wanted. In our heads, we wanted strings and choirs and all this dramatic, cinematic stuff that we couldn't have because we were just two kids in a basement. In our heads, we envisioned *Fallen*, but we didn't have the ability in the studio and we didn't have the ability as writers. We had a lot of growing to do." The duo did not let their limitations or lack of experience stop them, nor did they question their own unusual brand of music.

Ascension Of The Spirit

Toward the end of 1999, Amy and Ben strayed from their much-avowed exclusivity and invited one David Hodges to become a full-fledged member of Evanescence. "David is probably the only other person besides Amy that I could work with musically in this band," Ben told *Stranger Things* online magazine in a September 2000 interview. "Amy and I have always been so protective of Evanescence because it is our baby, but things just seem to naturally work with David. He is an incredible pianist and vocalist, and brings a lot to the table as far as production is concerned."

Ben and David would create the groundwork for the songs with the aid of Digidesign Pro Tools. They would then burn a CD for Amy, who would write lyrics and develop the melodies. "My writing is very personal. I have to go into this totally zoned-out dark place in order to write music. And for Ben, I believe it's the same way. He might write a skeleton for a song, and then I'll take it and go in my room sometimes for—I think the longest was a 10-hour stretch, and just, like, hash out melodies and lyrics and anything else I can come up with. And then, of course, some songs just flow out all on their own," Amy explained in the May/June 2003 issue of *Women Who Rock* magazine. The creative process was in high gear, and the band soon had enough material for a full-length album.

Meanwhile, local attention had spawned Internet support for the band, and quite a bit of cyber-hype preceded the release of an eagerly anticipated Evanescence CD. Fans were not disappointed. *Origin,* courtesy of BigWig Enterprises, was released on November 4, 2000, at a Little Rock River Market Pavilion gig that the band played along with Squad 5-0 and Living Sacrifice. The eleven-track CD was met with overwhelming enthusiasm and proclaimed even better than expected. It featured three songs that were destined to be on the band's future major-label debut *Fallen:* "My Immortal," "Whisper," and "Imaginary." For a limited-budget recording, *Origin's* sound was immaculate and a testament to Ben's dedication in the home studio. The many varied elements—piano, female vocals, heavy guitars, gothic and metal influences, electronic orchestration, synth programming, you name it—thrilled music lovers hungry for something different, something that actually sounded new. The scope of sound was truly impressive, and the buzz surrounding the band now intensified to fever pitch. Rave reviews cropped up on indie magazines and online. *True Tunes* magazine declared *Origin* "a stunning record" and predicted, "It will be absolutely shocking if this record isn't snatched up by a major label within six months of its release. It's that good." The addition of new member David Hodges was further augmented by guest spots from William Boyd once again on bass, vocals on "Lies" courtesy of Living Sacrifice's Bruce Fitzhugh and Stephanie Pierce, and a female vocal ensemble on "Field of Innocence."

Call it fate, call it inevitable, or call it plain old good luck, but it was while mastering demo recordings at Ardent Studios in Memphis, Tennessee, that a music-industry fairytale transpired. A producer by the name of Pete Matthews, who was working with the band Dust for Life at Ardent, caught an earful of an Evanescence session as he made his way down the studio hallway. His interest was sufficiently piqued to prompt him to knock on the door, introduce himself, and have a proper listen. His suggestion that he take the Evanescence demo with him to New York where he was scheduled to meet with various record companies was met with delighted approval.

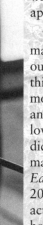

"So many times, so many people have gone out of their way to do things for us when no money was involved, or anything—they just loved our music and did things for us," Amy marveled to *Metal Edge* in its August 2003 issue. "We were actually mastering a homemade set of demos, and a guy named Pete Matthews, who was working on another Wind-up band and knows the label, thought it was great and went out of his way to meet us. About two weeks later, he told us he was going to New York and asked us if we'd mind if he pedaled the CD."

Independent record label Wind-up, whose most successful act at the time was rock powerhouse Creed, expressed an immediate interest. Next thing you know, Amy and Ben were on a plane headed to NYC courtesy of Wind-up—who apparently know a good thing when they hear it.

Amy recalled getting the word that a record company—a real record company—was interested in the band in a September 17, 2001, interview with the *Arkansas Democrat-Gazette,* saying, "I was at school. I was studying for finals on my birthday. Ben was in Little Rock doing things for the band, and I was all by myself. It was right before Christmas, and I was really sad. Then Ben called and said, 'Hey, you want to go to New York,' and I said, 'Yeah, right. I'd love to go to New York.' He said, 'No, really, like, we're going to New York.' And then I told him that I didn't have the money to go. I really didn't understand what he was trying to tell me." Little wonder. How many high-school students are whisked away from their studies to fly to Manhattan to meet with music-industry executives?

Wind-up, a boutique label known for its hands-on approach and personal attention, was a different kettle of fish to the long-established major labels. A prime example of Wind-up's dedication to its artists: The label provides health insurance for all of its artists and their families. "Our commitment is in developing real artists," chairman Alan Meltzer told the *Hollywood Reporter* in its November 6, 2003, edition. "We're not looking for an artist who has a really great song and then going in for the quick buck." Wind-up's interest forced the major labels to sit up and take notice, and competing offers started coming in, but Amy and Ben felt inclined to stick with the label that had believed in them from the start. Evanescence signed on the dotted line and Amy and Ben had themselves that golden ring: A record deal.

"All parents want their kids to go to college—do that stuff first and play in bands on the side—but once they realized that there was absolutely nothing that was going to stop us, they just accepted it. From that day forward they were very, very supportive because they saw how happy it made us," Ben told New Zealand's *Crème* magazine in a September 2003 interview. "The best [advice] was from my dad, who is in radio, but tried to be a rock star for a while. He said no matter what, always remember to have fun. It's not all about this business, it's about the music, so ignore the other crap," Amy told VH-1 in a May 29, 2003 interview. And if rock stardom didn't work out, Amy was prepared with a back-up plan. "I'd already started preparing for goal number two," she confessed in a June

2004 *Straight.com* interview. "I was going to go to music school and train to either write scores or become a music teacher. I love children, and I love teaching. And just as much, I love choirs and orchestras, so I wanted to learn the basics of all classical instruments so I could move into writing scores for indie films." As it turned out, Amy didn't need a plan B.

Live To Breathe

And so it was goodbye Little Rock, hello Hollywood as the young musicians packed their guitar cases and hightailed it to Los Angeles. Record-company contract in hand, they were eager to get down to business and record an album. Wind-up, however, wasn't quite so zealous, and suggested that the songwriting team spend a bit more time doing just that: Writing songs. True to their philosophy, the record company executives were in no mad rush to push the new band until they felt that they were fully developed. The label wisely felt that if the two teenagers could come up with material this good while attending high school—with all its inherent distractions—imagine what they could create given the time and the proper tools.

Steve Lerner, president of Wind-up Records, explained the label's perspective behind the wait to *Billboard* in its August 2, 2003 edition, saying, "The industry was not ready for an act like this when we signed them. We gave them the opportunity to grow, both as people and as performers. We knew we had found incredible talent." Alan Meltzer wanted to give the band an opportunity to mature both personally and musically. "We got them an apartment, gym memberships, a rehearsal space, and into the social scene and just let them go," he told the *Hollywood Reporter* on November 6, 2003. "We introduced them around to friends of ours on the West Coast—producers and managers—just to give them a feel for the music scene because it's a minefield out there."

Amy and Ben, though young, realized that navigating one's way through the notoriously tough music industry is dicey business. "It's more along the lines of trusting people that are working for you, or just understanding people's real motives," Amy said in a November 16, 2003 *Launch.com* interview. Luckily, in Wind-up they had a support system as trustworthy as they come.

Despite a bit of impatience, Evanescence took advantage of the opportunity afforded them by the label and blossomed. They continued to write new material and further develop existing songs. Amy took some acting/performing classes—after all, this was L.A.—in order to improve her stage presence "because I was really introverted and totally humiliated on stage," she explained to the *Washington Post* in its September 12, 2003 edition. "The acting helped because it was me alone in a room with a guy and I had to look him in the eyes and perform—it was the hardest thing I've ever had to do as far as that's concerned. Once I could do that and get over it and not be embarrassed to see myself, and have him tell me it looked good, I can perform in front of 100,000 people and I don't get nervous, which is really cool."

A bit more mature and with even more stellar material, Evanescence undertook what they only dreamt of all those years in their homemade studios and commenced recording the music they had envisioned for so long. The process began in August 2002 and wound up in December. They'd found just the man to help them realize their vision in producer Dave Fortman. As Amy put it in a *Straight.com* interview, "It was a fate thing—we'd met a few people, but it didn't click. Dave had produced a bunch of bands that sounded absolutely nothing like us... But when we talked to him, he knew exactly where we wanted to go with the record. We had a lot of elaborate stuff we wanted to do with choirs and strings and the way the guitars sounded. Pretty soon after meeting Dave, we were finishing each other's sentences. He just totally got it, and he made the record sound like it cost a whole lot more than it actually did." Formerly a guitarist for early nineties California pop-funk-metal band Ugly Kid Joe (whose *As Ugly as They Wanna Be* was the first ever short-form LP to go multiplatinum), he had produced for the likes of 12 Stones, Boy Sets Fire, Eyehategod, Soilent Green, and Superjoint Ritual.

It was Fortman who introduced the band to their manager, Dennis Rider. "[Dennis] is so great for us," Amy raved in a May 19, 2003 *Pollstar.com* interview. "We were all alone and frightened and didn't know what we were doing; we're just a bunch of kids. We met him, and it was like we just completely clicked from the beginning. He got it...and so did [Fortman]. They really understood our music and us." Rider was equally as enamored with Amy and Ben. "Sometimes, certain things just happen for a reason," Rider told *Pollstar.com*. "We all felt very comfortable around each other. Obviously, the stars were aligned on this alliance. I just love the band. To me, there's very little difference between the band as people and the band as musicians; their music is the same thing as their personalities."

Brought To Life

The band recorded and mixed at four different California studios: North Hollywood's NRG Recording Studios and Track Record Inc., Conway Recording Studios located adjacent to the historic Paramount Pictures Studio in Hollywood proper, and Ocean Studios in Burbank. For the first time, they didn't have to rely on electronic elements to convey the sound they wanted. "I didn't want it to sound too fabricated,' Ben told *Mix* magazine in it August 1, 2003 issue. "I love electronics and I love digital manipulation, but I wanted to first establish us as a real rock band. We're actually playing all of those parts: The strings are real, the choirs are real, the piano is real."

Ocean was the first stop, and Amy raved about her experience there on the studio's Website, saying, "Ocean Studios is the perfect environment for the recording artist because the studio becomes your world. I remember when we first came there our band name was on the screen saver of the computers, and it became the Evanescence studio. They treated us like someones even though we were no-ones. We recorded at many studios while making our album and Ocean stood out as being very unique. There's no other bands, no distractions, it's all about you. Thanks, Ocean!" Dave Fortman put his two cents' worth in as well, saying, "Ocean's got it all, great staff, beautiful sounding drum room, custom NEVE, comfortable atmosphere, and awesome attention to detail. I instantly felt at home. Excellent studio!"

NRG Recording Studios has earned its rocking pedigree having hosted the likes of Korn, Limp Bizkit, Linkin Park, and Godsmack, to name a few. The studio's distinctive look—featuring lots of wooden columns, walls quilted in satin and velvet drapes—is a small part of its attraction. Jay Baumgardner, who has been running NRG since 1991, had worked with several Wind-up acts including Drowning Pool, 12 Stones, and Seether, and aided Evanescence in the recording process during their month or so at NRG. Baumgardner, who mixed "Bring Me to Life," described the band as "sort of like Fleetwood Mac where everybody was a big talent" in a Trillium Lane Labs interview. The supportive vibe at NRG was just right for Amy and Ben. "In a way we sort of hand-pick the artists that work here, and find people early in their careers as artists and producers to help them out as much as we can," Baumgardner told *Digizine*. "It's a big melting pot here. We have barbecues and parties, and the atmosphere is always casual for everyone to have fun and get together. It's all down-to-earth here." Fortman, who had worked closely with Baumgardner in the past, had nothing but good things to say about NRG in an August 1, 2003 *Mix* magazine article, saying, "especially at NRG, everything you listen to and everything you record just has this bigger-than-life quality. That's definitely my favorite place to record. Jay just has the gnarliest monitoring system ever." Baumgardner also helped out in the guitar field by lending Ben a host of equipment such as Les Paul and Gibson guitars and a Mesa/Boogie cabinet that the studio head had used on Papa Roach recordings.

David Hodges is credited not only as a co-writer on every single track on the album, but he also played piano and keyboards and was responsible for string arrangements and some programming. Amy and Ben also enlisted the help of Francesco DiCosmo on bass and John Freese, a member of The Vandals and A Perfect Circle and a very busy studio drummer who has worked with quite a few bands from Chris Cornell to Guns 'N Roses. Soon-to-be Evanescence members Rocky Gray and John LeCompte also make appearances on the album—Rocky on drums and as a co-writer on "Tourniquet," and John as a co-writer on "Taking Over Me."

Achieving the lush, grand orchestral sound on the album was no small feat. A 22-piece string section provided the orchestral parts, which were recorded in Seattle by Mark Curry and then mixed in L.A. David Campbell teamed up with Hodges for the arrangements, with the excep-

tion of "My Immortal" for which innovative film-scoring heavyweight composer Graeme Revell was brought in. The 12-member Millennium Choir brought to life the choral element Amy had always desired. Amy, who wrote and directed all the choir parts, told *Undercover.com,* "Those ladies were so cool. It's funny because I was twenty at the time and they were between the ages of 40 and 55 and seasoned opera women and so I was like, 'Wow, you guys are awesome, that's so cool!' So I got in there and I'm the one conducting and teaching them." Fortman at times doubled the orchestral and choral ensembles, resulting in the quite remarkable depth on the album. When it all came together in the studio, Amy and Ben were literally brought to tears as they finally heard the beautifully lavish music they had imagined in their musical minds-eyes for so many years.

Evanescence then switched coasts and headed to New York City for the mastering process. Ted Jensen of Sterling Sound was chosen to master the album. Housed in Manhattan's Chelsea neighborhood, Sterling is an impressive 25,000-square-foot facility featuring eight mastering studios with separate editing and production suites, as well as a host of lounges. Jensen, whose extensive body of work includes the music of Metallica, Madonna, AC/DC, Creed, and many other top acts, is the studio's chief engineer and has been with the studio for some three decades. Needless to say, the band benefited from his talent and broad range of experience. Dorothy, we're not in the basement anymore.

Open Doors

In yet another twist of good fortune, "Bring Me To Life" and "My Immortal" were handpicked to be a part of the 20th Century Fox film *Daredevil* starring Ben Affleck and Jennifer Garner. "Fox was in love with our music, it was crazy," Amy told *Metal Edge* in its August 2003 issue. "I went to the soundstage where they were doing the scoring, and I felt like I didn't belong there. I was shocked, all these people like the director were around, and they were like, 'You're Amy? Oh my God! You're the voice of Elektra, your music makes our movie...' and I was like, 'Holy crap, what am I doing here?!' They wanted rock music with a female voice for her scene, and it just rocks."

Amy and Ben had always been interested in film scores, and now, as if by magic, their music had been deemed a perfect fit for a major motion picture. "It was an incredible feeling sitting in the theatre," Amy told *Popyoularity* in a February 17, 2003 interview. "It was really hard not to cry. One of the scenes that they used was a funeral scene. That's one of our oldest songs. It was written when we were in high school, early high school. It was mind blowing. I think it goes perfectly with the movie. We are just very flattered to be a part of a movie." Ben told Sony Music Australia on July 21, 2003, "It wasn't like we set out to do it, but it is kind of part of our style. We really love movies and we would love to write music for film and we also want our songs to be really descriptive and paint a picture and sort of tell a story. Which of course sort of comes naturally for us." Evanescence's particularly dramatic style was evident to Dave Fortman, who told *Mix* magazine in its August 1, 2003, issue that "One of the greatest parts of this record was the band's vision and their dream about it being theatrical and like a movie soundtrack. I think that gives it a special emotion, really. Every song takes you through this journey." Little did Amy and Ben know that they were about to embark on one hell of a journey themselves.

Radio station program directors begrudgingly aired tracks from the weird band with a female singer that obviously was not going anywhere after pressure from Wind-up. "There were a lot of radio programmers that took a while to come around and realize people are calling, wanting the song, and you have to play it," Ben told *Billboard* in its May 5, 2003 article. "A lot of people were like, 'Yeah, a chick, no place for her.'" The rabid response stations received from listeners who just wouldn't stop calling in immediately convinced them that in fact this weird band was most definitely going somewhere, and fast.

"We make our music the way we want to make it, the way we want to hear it. And if radio picks up on that then that's great, but it's not made with them in mind. We're an honest band, and the fact that we gel with things like that is something that just happened. But we do this for ourselves. It is not a contrivance," Amy said in a July 2003 interview with *Kerrang!* Magazine. "That's how it spread around the country, and around the world. That's my favorite part of the story—it happened not because we were being shoved down people's throats, but people were finding the band pretty much on their own. Who would we be without the fans? Nobody." Amy asserted on the band's website.

"Bring Me To Life" started hitting the tops of all of the U.S. singles charts, including, notably, *Billboard's* Modern Rock Tracks, very much a male-dominated chart. When "Bring Me To Life" made its leap to #6 at the end of February 2003 it was the first time in three years that a female-fronted group had entered the Top Ten. No Doubt's "Ex-Girlfriend" was the most recent interloper back in February 2000. "Bring Me to Life" soon hit that chart's #1 slot, and didn't stop there. The single went on to #1 on the Top 40 Mainstream, the Top 40 Tracks, and the Top 40 Adult Recurrents; and peaked at #3, #4, and #5 on the Canadian singles chart, the Adult Top 40, and the *Billboard* Hot 100 respectively.

The *Daredevil* connection was certainly a springboard for the success of "Bring Me to Life," but the song had a strength and power all its own. At the label's suggestion, fellow Wind-up artist Paul McCoy of the band 12 Stones was brought in to add a male vocal element to the song. His hard-rocking rap offered a fierce contrast to Amy's soaring, pleading, *"Save me from the nothing I've become."* The song's lyrics hit a chord with many brand-new Evanescence fans. As Ben put it on the official website, the song "is about discovering something or someone that awakens a feeling inside them that they've never had before. You discover there is a world that is bigger than just your safe bubble."

The video for "Bring Me To Life" beautifully captured the mood of the song. It depicts a slumbering Amy high, high above a gothic city in her bedroom. Disturbed by dreams of falling, she awakens, goes to the open window and is tempted outside by the night wind. A few floors above, in a room with padded walls, the band plays and Paul McCoy sings. Amy gracefully makes her way along the parapets of the gorgeous old building, and climbs up to the music above. The bridge of the song is dramatically rendered by a prolonged scene in which McCoy valiantly attempts to save Amy from plunging to the street below. The video's director, Philip Stolzl, told MTV on August 18, 2003, "I did not know if I would have to use a stunt double for most of the angles, which would have restricted me a lot, but then it turned out that Amy did everything herself, hanging on Paul's arm for hours without getting tired. In the end, she is the one who made that shot strong." The video was a refreshing change in an MTV world overrun with the same old same old of gangsta rap and teen pop, and it introduced a host of music lovers to that all-too-rare experience of discovering a new band with a truly unique sound.

No Shame

*M*ake no mistake: In a world inhabited by Britneys and Christinas there was no shortage of females in the music industry, but Amy Lee was an entirely different kettle of fish. She wasn't an alternative to rock, she was rock—heavy, hard-hitting rock full of in-your-face guitar that happened to feature classical piano, orchestral and choral elements, and a divine operatic female voice that was impossible to forget. Whether she set out to do so or not, Amy would make a major impact on views about women in rock. MTV was quick to take note that here was a chick who was going to make a difference, and its very first Evanescence news piece on April 9, 2003, was headed "Evanescence's Frontwoman Leads Rock Into Fem-Friendly New Frontier."

Amy discussed her experience as a woman in the music business during a June 2003 BBC interview, saying, "I really didn't face lots of problems, no uphill battles. We just never tried to make music that sounded like something else. The only struggle is very occasionally when people in the industry don't know how to treat you because there are virtually no other woman in rock—but people have mostly have been very respectful."

Her own female musical role models include Tori Amos, Portishead's Beth Gibbons, Bjork, Carole King, and Janis Joplin. Of Bjork, Amy told *Teen People* in its September 2003 issue, "I have every single thing she's ever put out. Her emotions are so complicated, just like all of ours. She doesn't try and dumb them down and make them pretty." Amy went on to discuss Tori Amos, saying, "I don't even know where to begin with her. She's an incredible writer, singer, performer—everything."

Not only did Amy rock with the best of them, she adamantly refused to use sex to sell her music. Yes, she is a stunningly gorgeous young woman. No, she doesn't feel the need to dress—or dance—like a stripper. "I respect myself, I always have," she told MTV on June 13, 2003. "I don't think there's any reason for some of the stuff that women celebrities do. It's a real shame, and it offends me because you're representing me. We're all women; we're in this together. And then they start to go downhill and people aren't paying attention anymore. So they start stripping their clothes off, because that's all they have left. I swear to everything I've ever known, I will never do that."

The themes explored in Amy's lyrics also set her apart from the majority of popular female artists of the day. Love, certainly, is addressed in many songs, but it is not a happy, sexy love but rather a tortured, at times suffocating, love. Pain, tears, screams, and deep dreams all feature prominently. "I go into a fog for a couple of days and lock myself up and work and it's usually somewhat of a dark place," she told *Rolling Stone* in its July 8, 2004 issue. "I'm a goofy, nerdy, normal person really, but I have issues, and the band's a place for all my issues. For me to be that dark character and hone in on the things that are wrong with me, that's where my inspiration comes from."

Eschewing the more banal themes often found in pop music, Evanescence goes straight for the emotional jugular. "I think our music is so passionate and emotional, whatever expresses a strong emotion, we're taking. It's definitely a bigger sound than just rock music, because we're pulling from so many places to get all that emotion into one song," Amy told *Metal Edge* in its August 2003 issue.

"The point of this whole record and band is to let people know that they're not alone in dealing with bad feelings or pain or anything that they go through," Amy declared in the band's official bio. "That's life and that's human. They're not alone, and we're going through it, too."

Paper Flowers

Fallen debuted in the U.S. on March 4, 2003 at an incredible #7 on the *Billboard* charts, selling over 141,000 copies in its first week. The little unknowns from Little Rock muscled their way into the Top Ten in the company of rappers 50 Cent, Lil' Kim, and Fabolous; Norah Jones and her armful of Grammys; R. Kelly; the Dixie Chicks; Kid Rock; and soundtracks to *Chicago* and *Cradle 2 the Grave*. *Fallen* would keep up the pace, selling some 400,000 copies in its first four weeks of release. For a band that pressed a scant 1,000 copies of its most recent release, averaging 100,000 sales per week ain't bad. "I never considered that people would respond to our music in such numbers," Amy confessed to U.K. heavy metal bible *Kerrang!* in its July 2003 issue. "I thought people would respond to the music, that there would be things

in it that people would attach themselves to. I think the music has those qualities; I think the lyrics are the kind that can help people through hard times in their lives. But the scale of it all wasn't something that I really thought about, not before it happened."

The album garnered unanimously stellar reviews. Critics across the board sat up and took notice. Here was a refreshing, new, genuinely talented sound—sadly, a bit of a rarity in the pop-music scene. "Evanescence's rich, guitar-heavy textures bring understated drama and allure to a genre crowded with sound-alikes," said *USA Today*. *Launch.com's* February 28, 2003 review proclaimed that Ben "could emerge over time as the guy single-handedly responsible for bringing back progressive rock with his heavy emphasis on atmosphere and Meat Loaf-meets-Rush pomp and circumstance." *Guitar One* magazine declared, "The Lee and Moody songwriting team have created one of the best heavy-rock records to hit the scene in quite some time—epic and progressive, yet loaded with hooks."

Evanescence, meanwhile, hadn't wasted any time waiting for rave reviews. They hit the road running, heading to Europe in March and early April to plant promotional seeds, a move that would prove to pay off in spades very quickly. They then set out on their own U.S. headlining tour—an impressive and courageous move. "It was weird going out on our first tour," Amy says on the band's official Website. "No one had any expectations, and we were doing a couple of shows in skating rinks for, like, 10 people—it was pretty hilarious. But by the end of the week there would be a huge difference every time, and by the end of the month we were playing to hundreds of people—and by last summer we were playing in front of 50,000 people in Germany."

In order to translate the *Fallen* experience into a live stage show, Amy and Ben elected to bring a team on the road with them consisting of John LeCompte on guitar and Rocky Gray on drums, and later added Will Boyd on bass. David Hodges had opted to leave the band to pursue his own creative interests. John and Rocky, both longtime figures in the Little Rock Christian death-metal music scene, had both been involved in bands Kill System and Soul Embraced. John also played guitar for Little Rock outfit Mindrage. "After Mindrage dissolved sometime in late '99, I got a call to play with Evanescence in Nashville," John recounted in an interview with the ESP Guitar Company. "It seemed like a good idea at the time, so I did. The show we did was a contest to win some equipment and

we lost, but we all felt the chemistry that we had live and decided that if anything were to happen for Evanescence in the future that I would be a part of it. We talked a lot that weekend about the importance of feeling like a family and not just having hired-on players to tour with. They are definitely like family to me and the chemistry after all this time is a fine-tuned machine." The multitalented Rocky, who had contributed drumming skills to early Evanescence EPs, was a guitar player for noted Little Rock metal band Living Sacrifice, as well as a previous member of Shredded Corpse.

Establishing Evanescence as a headlining act right out of the gate proved to be ingenious. Early gigs on the tour were raging successes, and aided the band in gaining their confidence and polishing up their live act. "I remember my stage presence used to be really, really bad," Amy admitted to MTV on April 9, 2003. "And then the more successful we've gotten, it's sort of just come a lot easier because I don't think that it's totally registered in my mind yet. I think I'm still kind of trippin' about it." Playing in front of large crowds in major cities night after night when your previous performances were rather intimate twice-yearly affairs certainly would be a trip, to say the least.

After years and years of creating music, to suddenly be catapulted around the world to perform was a shock to the system. Amy and Ben rose to the occasion with impressive zeal while fully recognizing the dichotomy. Ben told New Zealand's *Crème* magazine in a September 2003 interview, "Recording is a creative process. It's writing and it's very cathartic and therapeutic. It's a very necessary part of my life, but performing is just absolute adrenalin and almost selfish." "Being a writer and recluse and creative working in a studio versus going out, going on tour, being social, personable: It's like two completely separate lives," Amy reflected in a July 22, 2004, interview with the *Washington Times*. "I love the variety. But everyone needs to have that mix."

Heading out on a world tour before your debut album has even hit the charts was a gutsy move. The band's performing and promotion schedule was so hardcore that they could barely register the album's incredible achievement when it did burst onto the *Billboard* charts. "We were on tour when we first heard the album debuted at #7 in the U.S. Our manager bought us some Dom Perignon to celebrate. We've been working so hard—really I just wanted to take a pleasant nap." Amy told Sony Music Australia on June 4, 2003. There would be no time for napping, however—not for a long, long time.

Amy and Ben presented a united front to the burgeoning press interest in the band, conducting interviews and photo shoots together. Inevitably rumors began to circulate—and it was occasionally reported as fact—that the two were a couple, or, at least, that there was a history of a brief romantic interlude in the otherwise platonic partnership. "We have a great chemistry, like brother and sister," Ben told *Billboard* in its August 2, 2003 edition. "We fight like crazy, but we love each other, too. We don't go through a lot of stress and compromise when we're writing like a lot of bands do. We have a similar vision, because we love our music so much."

Evanescence touched down in Nashville, Tennessee; Louisville, Kentucky; and Norfolk, Virginia before hitting the one and only New York City. Here the band played a high-profile gig at Webster Hall, an enormous 40,000-square-foot landmark nightclub located in the East Village. The venue had, since its birth in 1886, been through many an incarnation, including the site of bohemian costume balls, a speakeasy rumored to be owned by mob boss Al Capone, an RCA Records recording studio, and a rock venue housing "the best stage in New York City." Everyone from Elvis Presley and B.B. King to Sting, Prince, Guns 'N Roses, and Eric Clapton had performed here, but Amy Lee and company didn't let that daunt them. They took the stage like seasoned professionals and put on a hell of a show, proving to a tough NYC audience that they had what it takes. MTV saw fit to review the gig, proclaiming, "Even the Spice Girls on steroids couldn't deliver girl power with such a wallop as Evanescence on Wednesday night in their first New York performance," and added, "singer Amy Lee piloted a packed Webster Hall with grace, charisma, and confidence—the latter surprisingly so, given that a New York audience can be daunting for a first timer." That under their collective belt, the band carried on through Pennsylvania, South and North Carolina, Florida, Georgia, Tennessee, Texas, and Indiana with barely a day off before winding down the first leg of their tour at the end of May.

It's like an old '60s 'love-in.' We're all having fun," Dennis Rider told *Pollstar.com* on May 19, 2003. "The tour is doing great; we're selling out nearly every night," he said. "We're not in shock because we knew we had something special, but it's still awe-inspiring just the same." The ambitious headlining tour was exceeding all expectations. The game plan was working flawlessly. "As we developed a strategy at the beginning of

Evanescence's career, we decided to move the band around the planet like a chess piece," Dave Kirby of The Agency Group (TAG) told *Billboard* in a May 1, 2004 article. "If you want to break a band, you have to move that band around. You only get people's attention for a moment, and you need to be there at that moment. No borders. If there is an opportunity to play in front of people, we go there." Quite something considering Amy Lee had never before traveled outside the United States. How often do you get your first passport in order to go on a world tour?

The band was offering up one hell of a show. As Ben told Sony Music Australia on May 20, 2003, "It's very theatrical, with special lights and Amy uses Victorian costumes and make up. It's a heavy brutal show, much more than you'd expect from the record. Every night I want to break something up on stage." The band was taking full advantage of the live performance arena to push the boundaries of their music. As Ben told *Billboard* in a May 5, 2003 article, the songs "just kind of grow and evolve as we play them live, day after day. Live is much heavier. It is the record turned up to 11, basically."

The Evanescence frontwoman was proving to be a consummate performer. Visually, she was a stunning onstage presence. Meticulous attention to detail produced an image all her own, complete with goth-tinged wardrobe and miles of impossibly glossy raven hair. Amy described her personal style to Sony Music Australia on June 11, 2003. "I wear lots of funky stuff on stage, I like to mix it up. I like to use two basic elements for my clothing—rock, you know, metal chains and stuff—mixed with fairies, drama, and Victorian clothing—fantasy." Her onstage presence is at once delicately feminine and powerfully confident. Her heavenly vocals are almost palpable and seem to soar above the audience. Despite the heavy nature of the band's shows, Amy was careful to treat her voice with respect and professionalism. "It's hard to express angry or bitter emotions and still be controlled, because when you're singing, you are being controlled. You have to think about what you're doing and not waste your voice," Amy explained to *Metal Edge* in its August 2003 issue. In a November 16, 2003, *Launch.com* interview, she expressed herself beautifully, commenting, "I love to sing because it feels like your spirit can talk."

Fallen Angels

While Evanescence had been rapidly expanding their fan base across the United States, a bit of controversy was a-brewing. Ben, exhibiting his usual candor during an interview he and Amy were giving to *Entertainment Weekly,* casually remarked, "We're actually high on the Christian charts, and I'm like, What the f*** are we even doing there?" In fact, *Fallen* peaked at #1 on the Contemporary Christian chart. This fateful interview—during which the band members have a tipple of alcohol, take the lord's name in vain (sample: Ben, when asked if there is any truth to the rumor that he and Amy were once engaged, replies, "Jesus Christ, no!"), and generally behave like any other twenty somethings—was to have quite an effect on the Christian music industry's take on the band. To further clarify Evanescence's feelings regarding religion, Amy offered, "There are people hell-bent on the idea that we're a Christian band in disguise, and that we have some secret message. We have no spiritual affiliation with this music. It's simply about life experience."

The message was crystal clear, and before the April 18, 2003, *Entertainment Weekly* interview even hit the newsstands, Wind-up was tripping over itself in high damage-control mode. In an April 15, 2003, article entitled "Evanescence Fall From Grace," *Rolling Stone* reported that Wind-up's Chairman Alan Meltzer took a pre-emptive strike and delivered a letter to Christian music stores and radio stations, in which he wrote, "Despite the spiritual underpinning that has ignited interest and excitement in the Christian religious community, the band is now opposed to promoting or supporting any religious agenda. The decision to release *Fallen* into the Christian market was made subsequent to discussions with and approval by the artist. Obviously the band has had a change in their perspective... Wind-up deeply regrets this situation." Wind-up's invitation to return the album and its offer to cover all shipping charges was met with swift accord. Big-time Christian music distributors Provident pulled some 10,000 albums off the shelves. Christian radio stations hastily removed the band's music from their play lists, and *ChristianRock.net* issued a sniffy statement declaring, "We have decided to stop playing Evanescence on our station because of their desire to not be involved in any way in the Christian music industry." So there. Media attention to the recall ran the gamut. Even the *Jerusalem Post* weighed in in its June 10, 2003, edition, asking, "Are they really Christian rockers or not? And does it really matter? Well, it matters to the extent that you can let your kids listen to Evanescence's major-label debut *Fallen*, and not worry too much about proselytizing." MTV took the most light-hearted approach hypothesizing that "Perhaps the chairman of Wind-up Records asked himself the eternal Christian query, 'What would Jesus do?' before making the decision to recall copies of Evanescence's *Fallen.*"

At the end of the day, Wind-up's decisive action seemed to satisfy everyone involved—luckily for the label that is home to several decidedly spiritual bands including most notably Creed. Pissing off the Christian music market just wasn't in their game plan. And being labeled a Christian band clearly wasn't in Evanescence's, so all's well that ends well. The religious controversy would continue to come up in conversation, however. When asked by VH-1 if she considered the band a Christian band in a May 29, 2003 interview, Amy replied, "I certainly didn't. Other members of the band did. We've always had our own beliefs. I don't think two people in the band think the same thing. In the past, other members of the band, who I won't name, stepped out of their bounds of representing the band and talking about their personal beliefs and it got thrown into the band's beliefs. That's not what this band is about. I don't want to alienate anyone. If you get a Christian message out of our music, cool, that works for you. We're just trying to write about our lives." Even at the end of 2003, Amy still found herself explaining away the Christian label. "In a nutshell, our music is spiritual, and my lyrics are very personal and about my heart and soul," she told the *Sydney Sunday Telegraph* on December 7, 2003. "The Christian market heard our music wasn't all about shaking your tail feather, that it was deeper, and they instantly assumed it was Christian music." Of course, Ben's declaration during a 2000 interview with online mag *Stranger Things* that the band's message was "God is love," his various religious-themed tattoos including a depiction of the life of Christ on his right arm, and the fact that first up on his *Fallen* thank you liner notes was a shout out to none other than Jesus Christ may have been ever-so-slightly misleading. "I have an intense history with Christianity," he explained to *Rolling Stone* in its August 2003 issue. Hey, what are you gonna do? Regardless, the confusion didn't do the band any harm—if anything, it may have generated a bit of extra publicity. Not that they needed it: Evanescence was exploding. Amy perhaps best summed it up to London's *The Evening Standard* in its June 12, 2003 edition, saying, "It's clear to me that our music is genuine. Sure, people are wondering about us, about our beliefs," says Lee. "Our band is strange, beautiful, and unusual, but we don't have to justify ourselves. Nobody writes our songs but us."

Screaming

*E*vanescence was fast becoming a worldwide phenomenon. The previously unknown U.S. band was suddenly topping charts in Spain, Germany, and England. On June 8 "Bring Me to Life" rocketed to the top of the U.K. singles chart, joining *Fallen's* #1 status on the *Music & Media* pan-European Top 100 albums chart. The band was in high demand on radio stations throughout Europe. Gerrit Kerremans, head of music at VRT Studio Brussels was quoted in *Music & Media's* June 14, 2003 issue describing "Bring Me to Life" as an "epic and dramatic song" and declared, "It's a new rock-rap-goth hybrid in contemporary music and it's certainly a significant single." James Curran of England's Virgin

Radio told *Billboard* in its August 2, 2003 edition that "For us, 'Bring Me to Life' was a breakthrough track, because it is the first single with nu-metal undertones that we have supported in such a big way. It has a commerciality which much of nu-metal does not have; it is a beautifully sung track with an incredibly catchy chorus." The band was also enjoying its fair share of European television exposure, appearing on the likes of the

U.K.'s venerable *Top of the Pops* and Italy's *Festival Bar.* Daniel Levy, vice president of marketing for Sony Music International, which has exclusive distribution of all Wind-up artists ex-USA, explained to *Music & Media,* "They have a good understanding of the international market and especially how Europe works. That obviously helps, but the reason they are doing so well is because there is just nothing like Evanescence at the moment. Both musically and emotionally they have taken rock to another level."

With word of mouth circling the globe, it was no wonder that the band began gaining new fans in all sorts of places. It was quite a surprise, however, when *Fallen* barreled right on to the charts in Japan at #1—a rare occurrence for an all-new international artist in that market.

Lee, Moody, and company decided to pay their British fans a visit, and signed up for the U.K.'s two-day Download Festival due to take place on May 31 and June 1. The festival, featuring over 50 bands including established big name acts such as Iron Maiden, Marilyn Manson, Sepultura, Zwan, the Deftones, and Ministry, also offered up quite a few up-and-comers, such as The Darkness, Funeral for a Friend, and HIM. The open-air, three-stage extravaganza held in Derby's Donington Park—one of Europe's premier Grand Prix motor-racing facilities—was a prime bit of exposure for Evanescence as some 50,000 music fans were in attendance. The gig was a standout on a personal level for Ben, as Metallica made a surprise appearance. "Kirk Hammett from Metallica is one of the reasons I play guitar," Ben enthused in a June 2, 2003, BBC interview. "I got to meet him and he actually knew who I was, and it flipped me out forever. I'll never be the same! He knew my sound guy, and when he told him who he was working for now he said, 'Oh, that's the only band I wanted to see today!'" Another landmark U.K. gig was the band's June 19 concert at the famed London Astoria. Evanescence went on to play scheduled concerts in Spain, but had to cancel a number of German dates due, reportedly, to Ben taking ill with dehydration.

Back in the States, the buzz was getting louder and louder. *Rolling Stone* took note of all the sensation, declaring, "this more-than-slightly anonymous Arkansas band has become the biggest new rock group in America,' in its June 26, 2003 issue, and observing, "As CD sales continue to evaporate, they are moving *up* the charts, one of the rare music-business success stories of 2003." Praise indeed.

Evanescence's legion of fans was growing with freight-train speed. Show after show was a sold-out, passionate affair, with packed audiences arriving expectant and excited and leaving thrillingly satisfied. Amy and Ben were themselves thrilled that the music they loved meant something to so many others. "Our fans are amazing," Amy told the *Syracuse Post-Standard* in its August 15, 2003 edition. "They're not going anywhere. We have good people all over the country and all over the world. In this business, I've seen cool fans, mean fans, and fickle fans. At the center of it all is a good group of people that understand me to some extent. Once you have a bond like that, you don't turn your back on them."

The band continued making house calls to new fans all over the planet and jumped on a plane for the grueling, endless flight Down Under. Evanescence was not about to let their Australian popularity go unnoticed. *Fallen* had debuted at no less than #4 on the Australian ARIA charts in mid-May, the same week that "Bring Me To Life" reached the #1 spot on the Aussie singles charts. A brief promotional tour of Australia involved live performances on nationwide stations Channel V, Rove Live, and Triple M. The band visited main Oz cities Sydney and Melbourne and gave fans a taste of the Evanescence live experience through in-store

appearances. By the time the band was settling in on the return flight, *Fallen* had reached platinum status in Australia.

The beginning of August saw Evanescence performing at the Teen Choice Awards (Ben showcasing his sense of humor by gamely sporting an "I Love Alyssa Milano" T-shirt) and picking up a Choice Music Rock Track award. Later that month Evanescence was awarded the Best International Newcomer award at the 2003 *Kerrang!* Awards ceremony held at London's Royal Lancaster Hotel.

Evanescence then took the headlining slot on the Nintendo Fusion Tour, a marketing executive's idea of the year. Nintendo set up GameCube kiosks throughout the concert venues, introducing new video game characters and showcasing old favorites. *Billboard* announced the tour in its June 24, 2003 edition, quoting Amy as saying, "We're really looking forward to doing this tour. When we're on the road, we play music all night and Nintendo all day. This tour lets us bring two of our favorite things together." "For me it just made sense to give people more of a good time...It's just more entertainment," Ben reasoned to AP on August 11, 2003. Joining Evanescence on the tour was Cold—who had just pulled out of Lollapalooza—Revis, Cauterize, and Finger Eleven. The 20-date Nintendo/Evanescence extravaganza kicked off at Los Angeles' Universal Amphitheatre on August 4.

The band capped off a tour-heavy August with a memorable appearance at Mountain Jam at the Denver's legendary Red Rocks Amphitheatre on the 30th. Also on the strong-armed bill were Korn, POD, 50 Cent, Run-DMC's DMC, Groove Armada, Gov't Mule, and Toots and the Maytals. The massive event also featured a DJ stage, skiing and snowboarding demonstrations, and the requisite chill-out lounge, just in case it was all too much to handle.

After months of near-constant touring, the band was now a bit more seasoned, and Evanescence's onstage performances were as tight as could be. They were fast developing a well-earned reputation as one of the hottest bands on the concert circuit and a must-see for a wide range of music fans. Men, women, kids of all ages, rockers, punks, classical music-lovers, choir dorks, metalheads, ravers—they all turned up in droves. It seemed that Evanescence had something to offer that transcended the usual boundaries.

Depths

"Going Under" was chosen as the band's sophomore single. A full-frontal assault of a song that leaves listeners catching their breath after its kick-ass denouement, it showcased Amy's vocal range and strength as well as Ben's guitar muscle. In true Evanescence style, heartbreakingly gentle cascading piano harnesses all of the song's brutal power.

The lyrics are about coming out of a bad relationship," Amy told Sony Music Australia on July 11, 2003. "And when you're at the end of your rope, when you're at that point where you realize something has to change, that you can't go on living in the situation that you're in. It's cool.

It's a very strong song." The emotional chorus *(I'm going under / Drowning in you / I'm falling forever / I've got to break through)* is portrayed in the video by Amy plummeting through the depths of the ocean. Translucent jellyfish echo the tendrils of fabric in Amy's shredded white gown, which she designed and made herself. The live performance segments of the video—in front of a crowd of ghouls and monsters—show a

glamorous Amy in an elaborate gothic outfit featuring a corset of her own design. The video was shot in Berlin by director Philip Stolzl, the man behind the breakthrough "Bring Me to Life" clip. Stolzl had worked with the likes of Madonna, Garbage, and Faith No More, but was best known for his many Rammstein music videos. The dramatic visual image of Amy's underwater scene would prove to be an enduring one, and further cemented the band's cutting-edge reputation.

The 2003 MTV Video Music Awards, held at New York City's Radio City Music Hall on August 28, would recognize Evanescence's repute. The band was nominated in two categories for the "Bring Me to Life" video: Best New Artist in a Video and Best Rock Video. They found themselves up against winner 50 Cent, All-American Rejects, Kelly Clarkson, Sean Paul, and Simple Plan in the New Artist category, and were beaten out by Linkin Park along with fellow contenders Good Charlotte, Metallica, and the White Stripes in the Rock category. Evanescence did however, win a Best New International Artist trophy at the October 23 MTV Video Music Awards Latino America.

The band hardly sat back and basked in the glory. True to hardworking form, they barely stopped touring, canvassing the United States with Finger Eleven, Cold, and Revis and playing in front of sold-out crowds in all over the U.S. of A. And then, lest Europe feel neglected, Evanescence crossed the Atlantic once more to keep the fires stoked. The band cut an impressive path across the continent. They played three concerts in Spain, going onstage in Lisbon on October 7, Madrid on the 8th, and Barcelona on the 9th. A couple of days off were followed by an Italian gig in Milan and a show in Switzerland at Zurich's Halenstadion. October 16 saw the band playing at Paris' famous venue, the Zenith. The band carried on performing to crowds in Cologne, Germany; Tilburg, the Netherlands; Copenhagen, Denmark; and Stockholm, Sweden.

Then the unthinkable happened. The tour was a rousing success and still had a dozen European dates left when Ben suddenly flew the coop—literally. The morning of the band's October 24 Berlin concert found his hotel room empty. The U.K. music magazine *Rock Sound* claimed to have the exclusive scoop in a November 2, 2003 article headlined "Evanescence Guitarist Walks Out." The shocking article disclosed that the band had been playing without Ben since he packed his bags and flew home to Little Rock with nary a word to anyone. The magazine quoted an "angry, emotional" Amy as saying, "You don't do that to your band. You wouldn't do that to your friends or your family. You don't do that to anyone." The *Rock Sound* article prompted news stories from MTV and *Rolling Stone* the very next day. Evanescence fans around the world wondered what on earth had prompted Ben's actions, and worried about the future of the band.

It was later disclosed that Amy and Ben had discussed parting ways, but hadn't actually decided who would leave the band—or when. Ben's choice of timing was not ideal from Amy's point of view. She would months later tell MTV in a February 26, 2004 interview, "It wasn't a big surprise that Ben was going to do something spontaneous and weird. That's pretty much how he is. He's going to do whatever it takes just to shock everyone. It's all about shock value, which is sometimes funny, I guess, but usually it's just a bunch of extra stress that nobody needs." Ben contends that he realized that his unhappiness was affecting everyone around him and that he just couldn't be responsible for the bad vibes one day longer. His shocking exit was not entirely unannounced; he telephoned Alan Meltzer to inform him that he had purchased a plane ticket home. The two men reportedly had a very long heart-to-heart, and Ben got on the plane feeling confident that he had made the right decision.

Meanwhile, the band continued to play without their lead guitarist, finishing up the European leg of their tour with an additional ten scheduled concerts in Germany, Scotland, England, and Wales, winding up with a two-night stretch at London's Hammersmith Apollo on November 8th and 9th. John did double-duty on guitar onstage. Meanwhile, Ben was spotted hanging out at Juanita's back in Little Rock. Concert reviews didn't seem to note the missing band member until Amy announced onstage at the October 30th U.K. gig at Manchester's Apollo Theatre, "Ben has flown home. But we're not going to cancel another tour so here we are!" This prompted speculation that the European concerts the band had canceled earlier in the year were not in fact due to Ben falling victim of "dehydration" but rather may have been the result of a previous falling-out.

On November 5, 2003, Associated Press published a terse quote from Wind-up spokesman Steve Karas who said simply, "Ben is not on the current dates." Evanescence then issued a statement on their website reading "Ben Moody has left the Evanescence tour and returned home. The band will continue touring without Ben and have brought in a guitarist to fill the spot. The tour will continue as planned when the band return to the States." Amy told Australia's *Sunday Telegraph* in its December 7, 2003 edition, "We decided there was no reason to terminate the band. It's evolved so much from when it was just Ben and I. I've been writing with the other guys. I'm really proud of the band."

Fragile Things

And so it was that the charming and charmed story of the two teenaged songwriters who made their dream come true came to its non-fairytale ending. The musical and personal alliance between Amy (who, in *Fallen's* liner notes, thanks "Ben, my best friend—for seeing me across a crowded room,") and Ben (who ended his thank you list with, "Amy, my best friend. You will always have 'all of me.'") was over.

As time went by it became apparent that things had not been quite as picture perfect as we'd been led to believe. "I actually haven't had any contact with him at all," Amy told MTV on November 17, 2003, some three weeks after Ben's sudden exit. "But I hear he's way happier, and I

know we all are, so it's for the best. It was just kind of an unhealthy situation for everybody. Everyone was really unhappy. I think it was just time to evolve."

"It was really strange on stage, as I'd never performed without Ben, but the feelings of uneasiness in our band had been so great, something had to

change. I think this has been positive for everyone," Amy told Australia's *Sunday Telegraph* in its December 7, 2003 edition. She also disclosed to the *Sydney Morning Herald* that, "The first show we played without Ben was sort of strange and weird and highly stressful. But when it was over, we had a really big party because we just felt this huge sense of relief—that we could do it without him. And it wasn't the end of the world and our lives would continue. Nobody died, y'know."

But what went wrong? Clues would surface in the months to come as the two former musical partners were interviewed and, inevitably, asked that very question. It seems that Amy and Ben's entire approach to their music, once so cohesive and single-minded, had split down the middle. Even songwriting, the foundation of their friendship, had become a bone of contention. Amy harkened back to their early days of creating music in a February 26, 2004 MTV feature, saying that back then songwriting "became this ridiculous fun thing. We put stuff in that wouldn't necessarily be anything like what we were hearing at the time. It would just be what we wanted because ... just because. It was never about boundaries or rules or follow-ing what somebody else did." Ben's countering argument was, "I made the rules very strict. It had to fit certain criteria...Just because something's catchy doesn't mean you're selling out, and just because you sell records doesn't mean you're selling out. And that was the word of the day with Amy. Sell-out this and sell-out that, and I'm like, 'Give me a f***in' break.' Just because you follow certain rules of songwriting doesn't mean you did something bad. It means you're a professional and you know what you're doing."

The professional in Ben and the artist in Amy were not on the same page. She expressed her frustration with his method in a 2004 interview with Australia's *Undercover.com,* saying, "Under Ben it was a really strict regime, you do everything exactly to measure and I don't believe in that. I believe in the heart of music, that's what music is supposed to be. It's not supposed to be dictated that way, it's supposed to be in your heart." Over and again, she expressed these sentiments, declaring, "It is all about the passion for the music." Amy asserted in a February 17, 2003 interview with *Popyoularity,* "It shouldn't be about business, technical stuff, or rules. It should just be about love for the music. We are music lovers. I love my job. I love music more than anything on earth."

Sudden success and fame is not, so we've all heard, the easiest of things to handle. Ben's outlook with regard to the music industry differed radi-cally from Amy's. Amy, according to Ben, was "obsessed" with being an artist, and loathe to deal with the business trappings of it all. Ben on the other hand was happy to join in. "There are certain things about the music business that, honestly, are not about music, and they're not about art," he reasoned to MTV on February 26, 2004. "They're about playing the game so that you can continue to stay successful, and Amy didn't want to play those games. I was more about doing what I had to do to be able to play music and do these sorts of things for a living." On the other side of the tennis net, Amy told *Launch.com* in a November 16, 2003 interview, "I would love to just have nothing to do with the business of this. I just wanna be an artist, and just sit around and make art, and let people listen to it. It's not about getting paid for me." As Amy told the *Sarasota Herald Tribune,* Ben "was kind of controlling, and in addition to that, he just became outwardly unhappy. So it was difficult for anyone to have a good time when there's one sticking out unhappy, not letting any-one else be happy."

Not Broken

*E*vanescence made its first U.S. appearance sans Ben by performing at the 31st Annual American Music Awards, held on November 16 in L.A. at the Shrine Auditorium. They pulled Terry Balsamo, Cold's guitarist, in to help out. *Fallen* was up for Favorite Album; fellow nominees in this category were Norah Jones' *Come Away with Me,* Kid Rock's *Cocky,* and winner Justin Timberlake's *Justified.* Evanescence performed along with Pink, Sean Paul, Rod Stewart, Outkast, Britney Spears, Clay Aiken, and Hilary Duff. A highlight of the evening was host Jimmy Kimmel's show-opening ban on the thanking of God during acceptance speeches. "God doesn't watch television," he assured the crowd. "And if he did, he wouldn't be watching this." Amy made an apparent dig at Ben when asked during the preshow what superpower she would like to have.

Her answer: Wonder Woman's Lasso of Truth as she would like "people to be honest."

After playing a November 19 Mexico City concert, the band announced the postponement of two dozen U.S. tour dates scheduled for November 21 through December 7, no doubt due to Ben's unexpected absence and the need to regroup and strategize. They did however say that they would honor three Canadian gigs set for December 12, 13, and 14 in Montreal, Quebec City, and Mississauga, and that Terry Balsamo would be Ben's temporary touring replacement for the near future. Ben and Amy still had not spoken. Amy seemed to be taking things day by day. "I think it's best to just let things settle for a while and do our own thing," she told MTV on December 23, 2003. "And Terry's just a great, easygoing guy. He's an incredible guitar player. He's good at everything he does, so we're totally glad to have him on the team."

Accolades and awards kept pouring in. Evanescence performed at the 2003 Billboard Music Awards held on December 10 at the MGM Grand Garden Arena in Las Vegas. The band triumphed over Beyonce, Chingy, and Justin Timberlake in the New Group/Artist of the Year category, and also took home the Soundtrack Single of the Year award. Evanescence was nominated for Best New Act, Best Group, and "Bring Me To Life" for Best Song at the December 2004 MTV Europe Awards.

In January Evanescence won International Breakthrough of the Year at the 5th annual 2004 French NRJ Music Awards in Cannes.

Fallen produced its third single with "My Immortal" which debuted at #7 on the U.S. singles charts on December 15. *Billboard* declared the song "a moving, piano-driven masterpiece that showcases a daring, soft side of the goth-metal band" in its November 1 review of the song. The single version of the song is not the same as the version on the album. Wind-up had chosen to use the band's demo rendition of the song on *Fallen*, rather than a later recording that the band preferred. The demo/album take on the song is a stripped down one, featuring only Amy and Ben and allegedly recorded in the middle of the night when the two "broke in" to a recording studio. When the time came to issue the single, the band won out and convinced their label to use their chosen version, which features a string section arranged by Beck's father, David Campbell. The song's lyrics were, unusually, penned by Ben, and Amy expressed her views about this in a November 5, 2003, MTV interview, saying, "That's the difference between us. Ben tends to write like a storyteller, and it's not necessarily from any kind of personal experience. I can't bring myself to write about anything I don't understand completely. For me, writing is always about some specific thing that's happened, so sometimes I feel a little distanced singing the song, but I still love it."

"My Immortal" exposed radio listeners and MTV viewers to a completely new facet of the hard rocking band they thought they knew. The lush ballad topped many U.S. charts and charts worldwide. The song also made landmark strides in cyberspace; *Billboard* announced on June 12, 2004 that "My Immortal" was officially the best-selling sheet music download of all time.

While in Barcelona just prior to Ben's jumping ship, the band filmed the video for "My Immortal" in a suitably gothic, older section of the city. It is an eerily prophetic clip. "The video is all about separation," Amy told MTV on November 5, 2003. "I wanted it to depict real human sadness." And that it certainly does. The beautifully shot black and white short seems, with hindsight, to depict the imminent break-up of these two best friends. Ben sits at the piano, head in hand, looking for all the world as though he is agonizing over leaving the band. The sorrow in Amy's voice is convincing as she sings, "*And if you have to leave / I wish that you would just leave.*" Ben's aforementioned album thank you to Amy is eerily echoed in the line, "*And I've held your hand through all of these years / But you still have all of me.*" Watching the video after the split was quite a poignant experience.

Despite the band's insanely busy schedule, Amy had managed to find a bit of time for herself, and had been dating Shaun Morgan, lead singer for Wind-up act Seether. And so, when the holidays came around, Amy took advantage of the break and spent time in Shaun's native South Africa. Shaun, the child of an English father and an Afrikaans mother, had formed an unsuccessful series of bands in his homeland before hitting upon a winner in Saron Gas. The rock group's heavy-hitting 2000 album *Fragile* was a huge seller in South Africa. Ready to conquer the world, Shaun and the band packed their bags and headed first to Europe and then to New York, where they signed a record deal with Wind-up and rechristened themselves Seether. Amy revealed to *Rolling Stone* on March 10, 2004, that when she and Shaun first began dating they disguised themselves in order to mingle with the audience at a Staind concert. "It was us being together, in the crowd, with all of these fans of Staind and us and everybody and they didn't know it was us. It was so amazing to be anonymous and remember what it's like to be a kid and love music," she enthused.

The band wrapped up their individual New Year's celebrations and jetted off on yet another whirlwind leg of their seemingly never-ending world tour. This time they were heading Down Under to follow up their first promo-only visit to the sub-continent in the summer of 2003 with a full-on concert-filled assault. They first stopped off at Australia's neighboring country New Zealand for a January 8 gig at Auckland's Town Hall.

The Australian release of third single "My Immortal" was timed to coincide with the band's arrival on the Aussie shores, and by the time

Evanescence hit the stage at Brisbane's Convention Center on January 10, *Fallen* had been certified triple platinum by the country's ARIA. Evanescence then headed to Australia's biggest city, Sydney, to play two sold-out nights in a row at the Hordern Pavilion on January 11th and 12th. Three more Australian dates followed, as Evanescence gained new fans and satisfied old ones in Adelaide, Melbourne, and Perth. The six shows had a strong impact, catapulting *Fallen* straight back into the national Top Ten at #6.

After satisfying their Australian fans' hunger for the live Evanescence experience, the group headed to Japan for an ambitious ten-date tour involving multiple nights in some cities. They played in Sapporo, Sendai, Tokyo, Nagoya, and Osaka, but the standout gig most certainly had to be their appearance at the Sonicmania festival on January 31 in Osaka and February 1 in Tokyo where they joined a hot bill featuring Korn, Finch, and Slipknot. "The biggest difference is between Japan and the rest of the world," Amy told *Billboard* in its May 1, 2004 edition. "They're so respectful of what you're doing, and they pay attention to every little cough."

No longer little-known upstarts, Evanescence didn't need to concern themselves with making anyone pay attention. They had survived the departure of the band's cofounder and soldiered on. It was clear that Evanescence was here to stay.

The White Forest

*M*eanwhile, reports were surfacing that Ben Moody had re-entered the music scene via an unexpected route: Teen pop. Ben was fast becoming the man of the moment for young pop stars looking for songwriting services and an infusion of rock. First up was 19-year-old Avril Lavigne, with whom Ben worked on the follow-up album to her smash debut *Let Go*. Exactly how the unlikely collaboration came about is unclear. It was alternately reported that it was initiated entirely by Ben, who contacted Avril's team and offered up his songwriting talents, or that producer Don Gilmore—who had previously worked with the likes of Good Charlotte and Linkin Park—had recruited Ben. Either way, the creative partnership was a success, and Avril's sophomore effort *Under My Skin* featured a Lavigne/Moody-penned song entitled

"Nobody's Home." Ben was enthusiastic and full of praise with regard to his experience with Avril, telling *Billboard* in its February 17, 2004 issue, "Avril can write songs faster than both Amy and me. I would just start playing and she would come up with these killer melodies and the most clever hooks. It's just ridiculous," He also weighed in on the Avril situation on his website, *benmoody.com*, saying, "Avril is a *very* talented writer. In fact, it was one of the most pleasant experiences of my career. She has been pigeonholed as a puppet, who doesn't write her own material and all that jazz and it just isn't true. In fact, I can thank Avril for a lot of upcoming Ben Moody music, because it was working with her that broke a 12-month streak of writer's block for me."

Next in line for a bit more edge was American Idol sweetheart Kelly Clarkson. "Let's face it, everyone wants to rock, it's just that some people aren't allowed to on their first record," Ben went on to explain to *Billboard*. "We're born to do it. If you have an entire record without a guitar anywhere, that shouldn't be legal. It's cool because [Kelly] wants to do some branching out, and I'm doing nothing but branching out."

Ben was indeed branching out, and not only with reigning pop princesses. He had begun venturing into film-music territory, something he had aimed to do for some years. The Ben Moody track "The End Has Come" on which he worked with Godhead singer Jason Miller, new Drowning Pool singer Jason Jones, and Living Sacrifice drummer Lance Garvin appeared on *The Punisher* movie soundtrack (which also offered up music courtesy of Puddle of Mudd, Nickeback, Queens of the Stone Age, Finger Eleven, and Seether featuring none other than Amy Lee). A songwriting reunion with David Hodges produced music intended for the film *The Passion of the Christ*. Ben also penned music for and assisted in the music supervision for *Resident Evil: Apocalypse,* and it was reported that Ben, in a partnership with *Resident Evil: Apocalypse* star Zack Ward, had established his own film-production company called Makeshift Productions.

To top it all off, shouts and rumors abounded that Ben would soon be releasing his own solo CD on Wind-up Records. It seemed that the Evanescence co-founder was content with his decision to leave the band and pursue other creative avenues and challenges.

Evanescence had an announcement of their own: Terry Balsamo was to become an official member of the band. He was a great fit. As Amy put it on the band's official website, ""Terry's a dream come true. He's a cool, laid-back guy that we've all been friends with. He's an incredible musician, a great writer, and an all-around five-star guy. I love him very much—there's no drama, it's more of a celebration than a struggle."

The news came as something of a shock to Balsamo's former band mates in Cold, and Amy's rather undiplomatic musings about the future of Cold to an Australian reporter didn't help matters. The Florida band that had been nurtured by Limp Bizkit's Fred Durst had released three albums since 1998. Amy speculated to *Undercover.com* that Cold "could hire another guitar player and continue, but I'm pretty sure that their lead singer is in and out of rehab and having real problems. He has been for a long time and I don't think they're going to be making another record. Terry was in a situation also where their band was very unhappy, so I think we came together on a common ground."

Ward responded to the news in a post on Cold's website, saying, "So it's official. Terry has left us for Evanescence. I don't know why and I don't want to. I also don't know why Amy threw my life out there like she did. I never did anything but treat her with respect. But this is the life I choose and I understand not everything can be a secret. I just wish she would have let me tell my story when I was ready."

Amy was quick to apologize, both on Evanescence's website and directly to both Cold and their fans in a post on Cold's website which read, "Dear Cold fans, I'm sure the last thing you want to hear right now is more of me running my mouth, so I'm going to make this short and simple. It was not my place to make statements about the status of Cold—Cold is not my band. I apologize. I've never claimed to be perfect and I'm not too proud to admit when I'm wrong. To the band: Sorry guys, I didn't mean to hurt anything for you. I'm new at this and I still sometimes forget that the world is listening."

Whisper

The world was indeed listening. Evanescence's incredible rise within the global music industry reached a quite fabulous peak on February 8. Sitting in the audience at the 46th annual Grammy Awards held at the Staples Center in Los Angeles with not one but five nominations up their collective sleeves, the band members surely took stock of all they'd achieved thus far and could only have felt an incredible sense of accomplishment. Either that, or a pinch-me brand of disbelief. "To have a Grammy would be incredible. To have any of those awards is incredible—especially so I can just let my dad keep them for a while. My dad is so proud. That's what those awards are all about: It's about your dad," Amy asserted in a November 16, 2003 *Launch.com* interview.

Everyone who was anyone within the music industry was in attendance, decked out and ready to party. Outkast, Beyonce, and Jay-Z topped the list of nominees. Conspicuously absent Janet Jackson, still in disgrace in the wake of her ill-advised breast-baring Superbowl incident, reportedly refused to publicly apologize on air for distressing the rock 'n' roll crowd and so was disinvited. Her partner in crime, however, Justin Timberlake, was happy to follow the rules and managed to keep a straight face while reciting, "What occurred was unintentional, completely regrettable, and I apologize if you guys were offended."

When the time came for the Best New Artist Grammy to be awarded, it was nominee 50 Cent who experienced a bit of disbelief. Evanescence was announced the winner of the award—widely considered to be the one of the most desirable of the evening—and the stunned and apparently pissed-off rapper jumped up, ran onstage, and exited backstage. How very gracious. Amy took it all in stride, accepting the award flanked by the band—including one Ben Moody—with a short speech, saying, ": Thanks 50! In addition to 50 Cent, I'd like to thank first of all my record label, Wind-up for finding us. Thank you to the fans because I know there's no way that modern rock would have put a chick and a piano on modern rock radio if it wasn't for the fans calling in over and over, so thank you guys."

Amy the next day weighed in on 50 Cent's charming stunt to *Rolling Stone*, saying, "I was in so much shock already, that that was kind of like, 'What?' I expected him to win, as well as I guess he did. I think basically it was a statement for him that he felt he should have won." It seemed that she was quite genuinely surprised that Evanescence prevailed. She told *Billboard* in its February 9, 2004 edition, "We've been nominated for a few different things, and I'm kind of used to seeing us up there and never getting anything. When they actually said our name, I was truly stunned." Aside from 50 Cent, the other nominees were Sean Paul, Fountains of Wayne, and Heather Headley.

Yes, that's right: Ben attended the show on his own, although judging by his appearance he wasn't taking a low profile. Dressed in an extravagant getup featuring a crystal-knob-topped cane and a long wig, he stood silently while Amy spoke on behalf of the entire band. Backstage, he entered the pressroom on his own to confirm his permanent departure from the band, commenting, "Amy and I spent eight years together. By the time we were 22 or 23, we were completely different people."

Amy looked stunning in a black and pink gown of her own design, made by Japanese designer H. Naoto and a necklace fashioned of metal-dipped twigs. She turned up at the star-studded event on the arm of Shaun Morgan. The *Arkansas Democrat-Gazette* asked Amy's father, John Lee, a disc jockey with KDRE-FM 101.1 in Little Rock, where the rest of the Lee family lives, about her choice of escort. He reasoned, "She wants to take her boyfriend. She's a normal 22-year-old," adding, "Actually, it's more fun to see her on TV from my living room in Maumelle without all the Hollywood glitz."

Evanescence also won the Grammy for Best Hard Rock Performance despite fierce competition from Audioslave, Godsmack, Queens of the Stone Age, and veteran rockers Jane's Addiction. The Amy Lee, Ben Moody, and David Hodges songwriting team was honored to be nominated in the Best Rock Song category. *Fallen* was nominated for Rock Album, and, incredibly, Album of the Year. What a night!

Pull

The band was straight back on the road for an additional fourteen dates in February, making up many of the canceled shows previously scheduled for November and December 2003 and honoring fans' original tickets. They started in Los Angeles and worked their way over to the East Coast for a hat trick of shows in New York; Washington, D.C.; and Boston.

Finally, finally! After a yearlong, nearly nonstop world tour that took Evanescence around—and around—the globe, the band took a well-deserved vacation. A proper break was surely in order after a year that had offered up many more milestones than most experience in a lifetime. The band members shook hands and parted ways for a record-breaking

two months. Amy and Shaun Morgan got far, far away from the rock star tour bus scene and reveled in a two-week South Pacific getaway. Early mornings and sun-drenched days on the beach were a far cry from the life they'd been living and were just what the doctor ordered. Mother Nature saw the couple out with a bang, however. As Amy told *Launch.com* on May 17, 2004, "We went to this remote island that you have to, like, take a seaplane to get to and all this stuff. And it was great because there was a huge hurricane the last day that we were there, and we had to stay an extra day, but it was really scary."

Unwilling to part ways and tired of conducting their relationship via transatlantic phone calls, Amy and Shaun made the unusual decision to tour together. With Seether as support to Evanescence, the couple could fulfill their performance duties and still spend time together—lots of it. Just before heading to Europe to commence the joint tour, Amy spoke to MTV on May 19, 2004 in a humorously entitled article headed "Your Bus or Mine?" and voiced a bit of concern, saying, "It'll be fun to see how it works. I'm gonna try not to blow it. Mixing business with pleasure: Sometimes it blows up in your face, but I'll try my best."

She may have been referring to the couple's prior collaborative experience. Amy and Shaun had previously done a bit of business/pleasure mixing by recording a song together. "Broken," a track on Seether's 2002 debut album *Disclaimer* was re-recorded as a duet featuring Amy for *The Punisher* soundtrack. The film's producers chose the song for inclusion in the film's soundtrack, but it was Shaun's idea to record an alternate version featuring Amy's vocals. "Amy and I have been dating for about a year, and when we both got off the road we decided to work together on it," he says on Seether's official Website. "We first recorded it in a Damien Rice, folk-rock kind of way, all acoustic guitar and cello. But then Bob Marlette expanded it more with the vocals and the strings, and essentially gave the song a facelift. At first I wasn't convinced, but part of the growing process is the willingness to try something new. It's now more exciting and emotional." The "Broken" video captures the song's theme of isolation, depicting Amy and Shaun in a desolate, wasted environment (which in fact was a defunct crystal meth laboratory that had self-destructed in an explosion). Despite the song's success, the couple decided in future to keep their collaborations the romantic kind. "I don't think it's a good idea because it definitely puts a lot of strain on our relationship," Shaun told MTV on April 23, 2004. "It's not something I'll do again because there are a lot of political things that go with working with someone. It goes beyond just creating something cool. It can become a nightmare if you let it. It's definitely tempting fate. All I can say is that I won't do it again."

Happily, the couple's latest collaboration generated only positive reviews. Once the tour was complete, Shaun raved about the experience on the Seether Website, posting, "That was really awesome. We've [now] been to countries that had never seen us before, so we're still seen as a 'new band.' There really was no better way to have presented ourselves to these crowds. We've already been invited back to several places—we've definitely left our mark."

The Evanescence/Seether tour kicked off on May 20 at the U.K.'s Hallam FM Arena in Sheffield. They then played Birmingham's National Exhibition Center before heading to London, where the May 24 show at London's famed Wembley Arena was a triumph. The enormous stadium was world-renowned and had seen every major musical artist in the last several decades on its vast stage. Evanescence managed to fill the vast space with their own huge sound, but it was when the beautiful black grand piano rose up to the stage from the pits below and Amy began to play "My Immortal" that the crowd was truly enraptured.

The two bands played throughout Europe through mid-June, touching down in Paris, Lyon, Toulouse, Montpellier, Nuremberg, Vienna, Rome, and Athens. Standouts were rock festivals in Germany and Portugal. The Rock Am Ring gig in Nuremberg saw Evanescence rock the crowd along with Korn, Motorhead, Machine Head, Funeral for a Friend, H-Blockx, Soil, the Datsuns, and Hundred Reasons. Surely Evanescence's biggest concert, size-wise, was the Rock in Rio Festival in Lisbon, Portugal. Tagged "world's biggest musical event," Rock in Rio for a Better World is also a charitable organization focusing on needy children. Far from an annual event, the festival first took place in 1985 and featured performances by AC/DC, the Go-Gos, Iron Maiden, Queen, Rod Stewart, and Ozzy Osbourne. It lasted ten days and was host to 1.38 million people. It apparently took some time to recover, as the next didn't happen until 1991. Ten years later saw Rock in Rio III in 2001. The six-day-long 2004 version of the musical extravaganza showcased all sorts of artists, from Paul McCartney and Peter Gabriel to the Black Eyed Peas, Britney Spears, the Foo Fighters, Evanescence, and Metallica.

Yet another single was issued from the album that just wouldn't stop selling. "Everybody's Fool" was *Fallen's* fourth single. "My little sister was really getting into these, I don't want to offend anyone, but like really fake, cheesy, slutty female cracker-box idols, and it really pissed me off. She started dressing like them and she was like eight years old. So I gave her the talk and I wrote a song." Amy told MTV on June 10, 2004. "Everybody's Fool" makes a statement about the futility in selling your soul in order to gain approval, fame, or fortune. In the song's video, Amy rails against lies and phoniness, displaying impressive acting skills as she takes on various female personas. All alone in the end, she sobs as she sings *"Never was and never will be / You don't know how you've betrayed me"* out her window to a giant billboard of her glamorous alter ego. The song's lyrics are visually portrayed very pointedly in this dramatic video.

The tour headed back to North America in July, picking up Three Days Grace and Breaking Benjamin as additional support and playing four Canadian gigs before hitting America with the five-band-strong line-up.

Amy treated a New York crowd to a piano-driven cover of Korn's "Thoughtless" at the July 22 Jones Beach gig. Live Evanescence performances often featured cover versions of some of the band's favorite songs. Imprinting other artists' music with their own inimitable style was a joy for the band and a rare treat for the crowd. Audiences around the world had the pleasure of hearing Evanescence perform Nirvana's "Heart Shaped Box," Soundgarden's "Fourth of July," Live's "The Dolphin's Cry," Smashing Pumpkin's "Zero," Garbage's "Only Happy When It Rains," Offspring's "Self Esteem," Stone Temple Pilots' "Sex type Thing," and Metallica's "One" and "Enter Sandman."

Throughout the tour Amy joined Seether onstage to perform "Broken," but she also enjoyed watching her boyfriend from the sidelines. "It's always an inspiration to watch the way Shaun works the crowd. It's almost intimidating. He has a way of getting people to just jump up and down, and he really just wins them over. I do things differently, but I'm 'performing' a lot more than I used to, to draw things out of the crowd and to rock harder. I've started trying to do that, but Shaun's still better at it," she told the *Arkansas Democrat-Gazette* in an August 13, 2004 interview.

The final North American leg of Evanescence's seemingly endless world tour was comprised of 29 concerts all over the U.S.A. and Canada, and it triumphantly finished up in a very appropriate city: Little Rock, Arkansas. The August 14, 2004 Alltel Arena show drew such frantic interest that an elaborate set of rules featuring wristbands and the banning of overnight lining-up at the arena was enforced. Who could have guessed that the band whose humble beginnings playing biannual shows to small crowds in the backs of restaurants in this very town would enjoy a sold-out grand finale to their triumphant world tour in Little Rock's biggest venue?

Where Will You Go

And so Evanescence, after an incredible journey full of surprises, does just what the band's name has been threatening all along and disappears—temporarily—to create yet another musical soundscape and evolve to the next level. Amy, John, Will, Rocky, and Terry dispersed to their own corners to begin individual songwriting with a plan to reconvene when they were good and ready.

"What's cool is that since the first album did so well, we have the opportunity to just relax and go away and hibernate and come up with fresh music. It's so important to have a great second album, and we'll take as long as it takes to make it perfect. If it's next year, or even the end of next year, so be it," Amy told the *Arkansas Democrat-Gazette* in an

August 13, 2004 interview.

All five of the band members would be contributing to the creative process this time around. "I think it's important for a band to all feel like they've invested their heart in the project," Amy explained in a 2004 *Undercover.com* interview. "Before what happened was the rest of the guys were brought into the band after it was already recorded, so it wasn't like they had their heart into it. We taught them how to play and they played it. [Now] we've been writing together and everyone feels like they have the chance to be in a real band, not just a hired musician." After

their time apart, a collective collaboration will take place at Amy's California home. "What I realized is that I have a band full of great musicians and writers. Everybody's kind of writing independently at this point, and we're going to throw it all in a big pot pretty soon and start writing together," Amy said in a July 28, 2004, *Teenmusic.com* interview.

It is an exciting time for the band, and for the fans as they eagerly anticipate the new album and speculate on what the sophomore effort will have to offer. "The next album won't sound so vulnerable," Amy told the *Sydney Sunday Telegraph* on December 7, 2003. "During the last album, I was in an abusive relationship. I don't want to go into details, but it lasted about three or four years. I can't even begin to describe how much I've grown in the past year. I've got a lot to write about." While the band was still in the midst of relentless touring, Amy was looking ahead and looking forward to getting back to writing. She told MTV on June 14, 2004, "I want to go in a lot of different directions we didn't go on *Fallen*. I want to get different emotions across. Obviously I think there's a spectrum of emotions on *Fallen*, but I think it's still limited in a lot of ways.... What's cool about *Fallen* is it really worked as a springboard, and we have the opportunity now to branch out and grow and do something different. I really don't want to put out the same album again."

Not least of those looking forward to the new album is Ben Moody. "It's going to be interesting to hear, because the only thing that's going to be similar is Amy's voice," he told MTV on February 26, 2004, raving, "It's going to be really, really good, because Rocky doesn't do anything unless it's good. Terry is a great writer. And Amy is an amazing vocalist. So you have all of the ingredients necessary."

How and when these ingredients are mixed, and what sort of musical concoction will result, is yet to be seen, but one thing can be certain: It will be as unexpected, inspired, and exquisite as only Evanescence can be.

1998

December 1998

- *Evanescence* EP is released at Evanescence concert at Vino's in Little Rock, Arkansas *(also reported as January 1999)*

1999

August 1999

- *Whisper/Sound Asleep* EP released

2000

November 2000

- November 4: *Origin* released on local Little Rock label Big Wig Enterprises at an Evanescence concert at the River Market Pavilion in Little Rock Arkansas. Squad 5-0 and Living Sacrifice also played the gig.

2001

February 2001

- February 3: Evanescence Saturday night headlining gig at the TNT Powerhouse in Bryant, Arkansas, with My Space Coaster as the opening act. Admission $5.

December 2001

- December 22: Evanescence Saturday night headlining gig at Juanita's in Little Rock, Arkansas with Blue Karma as the opening act. Admission $8.

2002

August – December 2002

- Evanescence record their Wind-up Records debut in California at NRG Recording Studios, Track Record Inc., Conway Recording Studios, and Ocean Studios.

2003

January 2003

- "Bring Me To Life" promotional single released

- January 13: Evanescence host a CD listening party and autograph-signing session at Juanita's in Little Rock, Arkansas, to celebrate the inclusion of "Bring Me to Life" and "My Immortal" in the 20th Century Fox film *Daredevil* starring Ben Affleck and Jennifer Garner.

February 2003

- February 14: *Daredevil* is released.

- February 28: "Bring Me To Life" is the first single featuring a female vocalist to crack the Top Ten of *Billboard*'s Modern Rock Tracks chart in three years.

March 2003

- Evanescence European promotional tour

- March 4: Evanescence's Wind-up Records debut album *Fallen* released

- March 12: *Fallen* debuts at #7 in the US with more than 141,000 copies sold

April 2003

- "Bring Me To Life" U.S. single released

- Evanescence U.S. tour

- April 16: Standout gig at New York City's Webster Hall

- Wind-up Records recalls *Fallen* from Christian music market

- April 18: *Entertainment Weekly* issue containing fateful interview in which Evanescence denounces any affiliation with the Christian music scene hits newsstands

May 2003

- Evanescence U.S. tour

- May 18: *Fallen* certified platinum in the US

- *Fallen* debuts at #4 on Australian ARIA album charts

June 2003

- *Fallen* #1 on *Music & Media* pan-European Top 100 Albums chart

- Evanescence European tour

- June 19: Standout gig at the London Astoria

- German dates cancelled due to Ben Moody falling ill

July 2003

- Evanescence Australian promotional tour

scence

Timeline

August 2003

- Evanescence headline the Nintendo Fusion tour with Cold, Revis, Cauterize, and Finger Eleven as support

- Evanescence perform at Teen Choice Awards and win Choice Music Rock Track Award

- Evanescence win Best International Newcomer Award at *Kerrang!* Awards in London

- **August 28:** MTV Video Music Awards–Evanescence nominated for Best New Artist in a Video and Best Rock Video for "Bring Me To Life"

- **August 30:** Standout gig at Mountain Jam at Red Rock's Amphitheatre in Denver, Colorado

September 2003

- "Going Under" U.S. single released

- Evanescence headline the Nintendo Fusion tour with Cold, Revis, Cauterize, and Finger Eleven as support

October 2003

- Evanescence European tour

- **October 23:** Evanescence win Best New International Artist Award at MTV Video Music Awards Latin America

- **October 24:** Ben Moody leaves Evanescence during European tour to fly home to Little Rock, Arkansas. His departure from the band is permanent. Evanescence continues European tour without Moody.

November 2003

- Evanescence European tour

- **November 16:** Evanescence performs at American Music Awards in Los Angeles; *Fallen* nominated for Favorite Album

- Evanescence cancels 12 U.S. dates

December 2003

- "My Immortal" U.S. single released

- **December 10:** Evanescence performs at *Billboard* Music Awards in Las Vegas and wins New Group/Artist of the Year Award

- Evanescence resumes headlining tour in Canada

2004

January 2004

- Evanescence New Zealand and Australian tour

- **January 16:** Evanescence name Terry Balsamo as new guitarist

- Evanescence Japanese tour

February 2004

- **February 8:** Evanescence win Best New Artist and Best Hard Rock Performance awards at the Grammy Awards in Los Angeles

- Evanescence U.S. tour

May 2004

- "Everybody's Fool" U.S. single released

- Evanescence European tour with Seether as support

- **May 24:** Standout gig at London's Wembley Arena

June 2004

- Evanescence European tour with Seether as support

- Standout gig at Rock in Rio Festival in Lisbon

July 2004

- Evanescence North American tour with Seether and Three Days Grace as support

August 2004

- Evanescence North American tour with Seether, Three Days Grace, and Breaking Benjamin as support

- **August 14:** Standout gig in Little Rock is grand finale of tour

Evanescence EP

Where Will You Go / Solitude / Imaginary /
Exodus / So Close / Understanding / The End
*BigWig Enterprises, December 1998 or January
1999*
Guest musicians are William Boyd on bass and
guitar, Matt Outlaw on drums, and Rocky Gray
on drums.

Whisper/Sound Asleep EP

Give Unto Me (Sound Asleep) / Whisper /
Understanding (Sound Asleep Version) /
Forgive Me / Understanding (Original Version) /
Ascension of the Spirit
August 1999

Origin

Origin / Whisper / Imaginary / My Immortal /
Where Will You Go / Field of Innocence /
Even in Death / Anywhere / Lies /
Away from Me / Eternal
BigWig Enterprises, November 4, 2000
Features David Hodges as band member and
guest spots William Boyd on bass, vocals on
"Lies" courtesy of Bruce Fitzhugh and Stephanie
Pierce, and a female vocal ensemble on "Field of
Innocence."

Bring Me To Life Promotional Single

Bring Me to Life
Wind-Up Records, January 2003

Daredevil Soundtrack

Won't Back Down (Fuel) / For You (The
Calling) / Bleed for Me (Saliva) / Hang On
(Seether) / Learn the Hard Way (Nickelback) /
The Man Without Fear (Drowning Pool featur-
ing Rob Zombie) / Right Now (Nappy Roots
featuring Marcus Curiel of POD) / Evening Rain
(Moby) / **Bring Me To Life (Evanescence)** / Until
You're Reformed (Chevelle) / Right Before Your
Eyes (Hoobastank) / Fade Out-In (PaloAlto) /
Caught in the Rain (Revis) / High Wire Escape
Artist (BOYSETSFIRE) / Raise Your Rifles
(Autopilot Off) / Daredevil Theme [Blind Justice
Remix] (Graeme Revell and Mike Einziger) / **My
Immortal (Evanescence)** / Sad Exchange (Finger
Eleven) / Simple Lies (Endo) / Let Go (Twelve
Stones)
Wind-up Records, February 4, 2003

Fallen

Going Under / Bring Me To Life /
Everybody's Fool / My Immortal / Haunted /
Tourniquet / Imaginary / Taking Over Me /
Hello / My Last Breath / Whisper
Wind-up Records, March 4, 2003

Bring Me To Life Single

Bring Me To Life / Bring Me To Life (Bliss Mix) /
Farther Away / Missing
Wind-up Records, April 2003

Going Under Single

Going Under / Going Under (Live Acoustic) /
Heart Shaped Box (Live Acoustic) / Going
Under Video
Wind-up Records, September 2003

My Immortal Single

My Immortal (Band Version) / My Immortal
(Live from Cologne) / Haunted (Live from
Sessions @ AOL)
Wind-up Records, December 2003

Everybody's Fool Single

Everybody's Fool / Taking Over Me (Live from
Cologne) / Whisper (Live from Cologne) /
Everybody's Fool (Instrumental Version)
Wind-up Records, May 2004